THE KIDS' GUIDE TO SPORTS ETHICS

BY CHRISTOPHER FOREST

CAPSTONE PRESS
a capstone imprint

SI Kids Guide Books are published by
Capstone Press
1710 Roe Crest Drive
North Mankato, Minnesota 56003
www.capstonepub.com

Library of Congress Cataloging-in-Publication Data
Forest, Christopher.
  The kids' guide to sports ethics / by Christopher Forest.
      pages cm.—(Sports illustrated kids. SI kids guide books)
  Includes index.
  ISBN 978-1-4765-4153-2 (library binding)
  ISBN 978-1-4765-5185-2 (paperback)
  1. Sports—Moral and ethical aspects—Juvenile literature. I. Title.
  GV706.3.F67 2014
  175—dc23   2013032844

Editorial Credits
Anthony Wacholtz, editor; Sarah Bennett, designer; Eric Gohl,
media researcher; Charmaine Whitman, production specialist

Photo Credits
Alamy: Joe Belanger, 28; AP Photo: Piqua Daily Call/Mike Ullery,
41; Corbis: Bettmann, 27 (top); Dreamstime: Mezzotint, cover; Getty
Images: Michael Zagaris, 33, NHLI/Jeff Vinnick, 22, Popperfoto, 39,
The Washington Post/Toni L. Sandys, 30; iStockphotos: AlexSava,
38; Landov: The Oregonian/Blake Wolf, 43; Library of Congress:
11; Newscom: AFP/Walter Bieri, 44, Agence France Presse/Peter
Newcomb, 27 (bottom), AI Wire/Jorge Lemus, 37, Cal Sport Media/
Eric Canha, 9, Icon SMI/John Cordes, 24, Icon SMI/Tim Vizer, 13,
Icon SMI/TSN/Albert Dickson, 31, KRT/Joe Rimkus Jr., 16, MCT/
Ethan Hyman, 32, Popperfoto/United Archives/KPA, 42, Reuters/
Bill Waugh, 21, ZUMA Press/Kirthmon F. Dozier, 36; Shutterstock:
bikeriderlondon, 14, Rena Schild, 5; Sports Illustrated: Al
Tielemans, 4, 34, 35, Bill Frakes, 8, Bob Martin, 29, Chuck Solomon,
25, Damian Strohmeyer, 10, 19 (top), 20, David E. Klutho, 12, John
G. Zimmerman, 40, John W. McDonough, 15, 19 (bottom), 23, Robert
Beck, 6, Simon Bruty, 17

Design Elements: Shutterstock

Printed in the United States of America in Stevens Point, Wisconsin.
092013   007767WZS14

TABLE OF CONTENTS

ETHICS AND
SPORTSMANSHIP

Sports have entertained people for ages. The solid crack of a bat smashing a game-winning home run. The work of an Olympian that pays off in a gold medal. The buzzer-beating shot of a college student that wins the national championship.

The U.S. women's soccer team wins the gold medal at the 2012 Summer Olympics.

At all levels, sports often leave us with pictures of hard work and dedication. Athletes practice and train before the start of a volleyball season. A player hustles down the first base line to beat a throw. Fans cheer the home team as the players hoist a championship trophy high.

But sports also present a lot of questions, especially for athletes. What is the right way to act on the field? What's the best way to train ethically? What unwritten rules are there to follow?

It's during such times that **sportsmanship** becomes important. There are no official rules of sportsmanship. However, many athletes hold to the idea of sportsmanship and ethical behavior—like an honor code to the game.

sportsmanship—the spirit of playing a sport fairly and to the best of one's ability

CHAPTER 1

Honoring the Game

UNWRITTEN RULES

➡ *During a baseball game, you swing the bat hard and hear a solid smack. You look up and know the ball is going to leave the ballpark. You want to watch the ball carry over the fence. But the pitcher is already staring you down.* **WHAT WOULD YOU DO?**

It might be fun to stand there and watch the ball leave the park. But the opposing team might feel as if you are showing off. Running the bases—and not stopping to watch your home run—is one of many unwritten rules in sports. Unwritten rules are basic guidelines of ethical play and good sportsmanship. But not everyone follows unwritten rules. People who break them can create hard feelings between teams.

RUNNING UP THE SCORE

Two teams that are facing off in any sport might not be at the same playing level. The game might end in a **blowout**. In 2011 Pikeville Junior High School in Kentucky played a basketball game against a smaller school featuring several younger players. Pikeville scored 25 points within the first two minutes, and the coach took the starters out of the game. Even so, Pikeville built a 70-0 lead at halftime and ended up winning 100-2. A Texas high school football game had a similar result in 2013. Aledo High defeated Western Hills 93-0.

Blowouts can happen, but sometimes poor sportsmanship comes into play. Adding to the score more than necessary, especially on trick plays, is frowned upon. Sometimes the coaches will keep their best players in the game to run up the score. To avoid a lopsided score, most coaches put in backup players to let them get game-time experience. After the game the winning players should respect the other players and shake hands without rubbing in the outcome.

blowout—a game in which one team greatly outscores its opponent

CELEBRATIONS

When athletes make great plays during a game, they want to celebrate. In the past National Football League (NFL) players would do group dances or include props during touchdown celebrations. Memorable celebrations include Chad Johnson of the Cincinnati Bengals pretending to give CPR to the football and the Carolina Panthers' Steve Smith making a snow angel in the end zone. But some people argue that celebrations take away from the touchdown and can insult the other team.

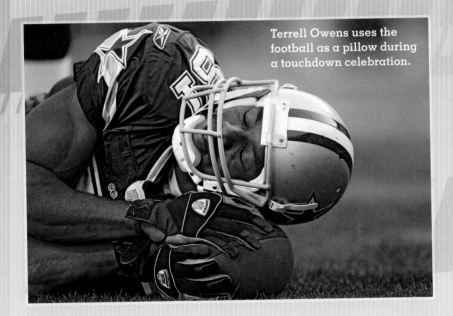

Terrell Owens uses the football as a pillow during a touchdown celebration.

Today the NFL has rules against excessive celebrations. Referees can give penalties to a team or player who celebrates too much. Whether a penalty will be called sometimes depends on how the action is performed. For example, players can spike the ball to celebrate. However, they can't spike the ball in the direction of an opposing player.

Alan Williams of the University of Massachusetts Minutemen somersaults into the end zone after a touchdown run.

SHOWING OFF

Showing athletic ability is part of the sport. But sometimes athletes can take things too far or perform unnecessary plays. In basketball a player might break away and toss a pass off the backboard before a dunk when his team is ahead by 30 points. A football player might run down the field alone for a touchdown. Before crossing the goal line, he might do an elaborate dive into the end zone instead of simply running in for the score. In baseball a runner might try to steal third base with his team up by eight runs. In each case the opposing players might be upset or think the other team is rubbing it in.

DANGEROUS HITS

In recent years, head injuries have been the focus for many sports leagues. The NFL has paid close attention to **concussions**, which has resulted in many positive rule changes. In football and hockey, serious penalties and fines can be assessed to players who lead a hit with their head. In baseball, pitchers should avoid throwing near the batter's head. In fact, pitchers who come too close to the batter's head can be thrown out of the game. In basketball hitting a player purposely in the head is often a flagrant foul. It might result in the player being ejected or even suspended.

In football, hits near and below the knees won't draw a penalty, but the player may be fined. Injuries can occur when a helmet smashes into the lower leg. New England quarterback Tom Brady sustained a season-ending injury because of a low hit. Blocks and tackles at and below the knee are subject to fines. Detroit Lions defensive tackle Ndamukong Suh received a record $100,000 fine in 2013 for a knee block on Minnesota Vikings center John Sullivan.

During the first week of the 2008 season, Tom Brady tore two knee ligaments after a low hit and missed the rest of the season.

Ty Cobb

SLIDING WITH YOUR CLEATS UP

Players in many sports wear cleats, which are footwear with metal or hard plastic points on the bottom. Cleats help the players grip turf. But they can also hurt opposing players. Athletes in baseball and football are expected to slide with their cleats down as best they can. While there are no rules against how players slide, it's a common courtesy to other athletes. If a player slides with his or her cleats up, the sharp points could badly cut the other player, which could lead to missed games.

concussion—an injury to the brain caused by a hard blow to the head

FLOPPING

➡ *During a basketball game with a rival team, you are the only defender on a 2-on-1 fast break. The player with the ball suddenly cuts toward the basket as you throw up your arms. Her body barely makes contact with you as she goes up with the ball, but she did have to go over you to make the shot. If you fall backward hard, you could probably get the ref to call a charge on her.* **WHAT WOULD YOU DO?**

Falling or faking contact is called flopping or diving. These actions are intended to draw a foul or penalty on an opponent. But with cameras capturing the game action, it's easy to watch the replay and see what really happened. However, that doesn't help the referees during the game. Flopping can make the referees look bad. It also makes the flopping player look like a poor sport.

Most players avoid flopping because they want to follow the code of good sportsmanship. Many sport leagues have rules to guard against diving and flopping. Players can be penalized or fined if the league determines he or she flopped. In the NBA players who break the rule have to pay a $5,000 fine for the first time they flop. The fine increases each time, reaching $30,000 for the fifth offense. After that they could receive a larger fine or be suspended.

A referee may call a player for charging if the defender flops.

FACT

In the 2012-13 NBA playoffs, two players flopped on the same play. In Game 4 of the Eastern Conference Finals, David West of the Indiana Pacers backed into Miami Heat's LeBron James. James hit the floor while West stumbled backward. No foul was called in the play, but each player later received a $5,000 fine.

STEALING SIGNS

➡ You are on second base waiting for the next pitch.
You see the batter step out of the batter's box and notice
the catcher making a motion to the pitcher. He's holding
up two fingers, followed by an L-shape. The last two
times he made that signal, the pitcher threw a fastball up
and in. Sure enough, on the next pitch the pitcher throws
a fastball. It is up and in—and your teammate strikes
out. Your teammate may have made an out, but now you
know what the symbol means. **WHAT WOULD YOU DO?**

FACT

In baseball teams frequently change signs during the game to prevent other teams from stealing them.

Most athletes think it is unacceptable to watch the signs of other teams. This behavior is called stealing signs. Some professional teams have accused their opponents of stealing signs. Some have claimed that video cameras have been pointed into dugouts to capture signs.

Stealing signs typically occurs in baseball and softball. Football and basketball players have also been accused of watching and stealing signals. It can happen during any game in which signs or signals are used to call plays.

Bill Belichick

The Patriots were accused of videotaping the New York Jets' signals during a 2007 game in what came to be called Spygate. The team was fined $250,000, and coach Bill Belichick received a record $500,000 penalty.

While stealing signs is often considered bad sportsmanship, being observant is not. Watch the way a pitcher moves or look at how a base runner stands. Is there something they do before making a certain pitch or getting ready to steal a base? If so, these players are tipping off their behavior. There is nothing wrong with using those clues to your advantage.

FAKING INJURIES

➡ *You are racing down the ice, hockey stick in hand. There are two minutes left in the game and you and your teammates are feeling winded. You could use a* **time-out** *right now, if only there was a stop in play. Suddenly an opponent bumps into you and you fall to the ice. You are about to get up, but you wonder if you should pretend to be injured. The ref will blow a whistle, and your teammates can catch their breath. Your coach might be able to set up a play too.* **WHAT WOULD YOU DO?**

Injury time-outs are designed to help players who are truly injured. Faking an injury to help your team would be unethical. In most leagues it is against the rules.

A referee raises his arms, signaling a time-out. Play stops so the injured player can receive treatment and has time to get off the field safely.

It can be difficult for a referee to tell if a player is
faking an injury or is truly hurt.

Some players still try to fake injuries. It can happen
in almost any sport. There are three main reasons
players fake injuries:

• Players might need to catch their breath and rest
  for a moment
• A player might try to throw off the tempo of a
  fast-paced team
• A team might need an extra time-out to set up
  a play or to sub in players

None of these reasons are considered valid for
faking an injury. In most leagues players can be fined
or suspended for pretending to be hurt. The problem
is that it is hard to prove someone is faking an injury.
Leagues often have to trust that players will not abuse
an injury time-out.

time-out—a pause taken during a game that can
be called by a team member or game official

17

CHAPTER 2

Player Interaction

RIVALRIES

> ➡ *You walk into the opposing ballpark nervous for the upcoming game. It's the first time you're starting against your team's biggest rival. The two teams have faced each other hundreds of times. Most games have been close. Even before the first pitch is thrown, players on the other team are taunting your team.* **WHAT WOULD YOU DO?**

Competitions between two teams that have a long, fierce history are called **rivalries**. Games between rivals can be a lot of fun, but they can also be problematic. Rivalries often bring tremendous competition, but some teams get carried away. A pitch aimed behind a batter, an unnecessarily hard hit, or a few taunting words can get the blood boiling on both teams.

When tempers start flaring, teammates help each other remember that the rivalry is based on competition. Don't hurl remarks back at the other team. Instead, try your best to win the game fairly and show sportsmanship to the other team's players, even if they don't show it back

Some of the most famous rivalries have spanned decades. "What would baseball be like without the Red Sox and Yankees?" Magic Johnson once asked. And Johnson should know. He and Larry Bird were part of the legendary Lakers and Celtics rivalry that has lasted more than 40 years. Bird and Johnson were friends, but they also took their NBA rivalry seriously.

Famous Team Rivalries
Red Sox vs. Yankees
Harvard vs. Yale
Celtics vs. Lakers
Army vs. Navy
Duke vs. North Carolina

Magic Johnson (left) and Larry Bird

rivalry—a fierce feeling of competition between two players or teams

QUESTIONING
THE CALL

➡ You are driving the lane during a basketball game when your opponent's elbow hits your shoulder and neck. The ball flies out of bounds, but the refs don't call a foul, and the other team gets the ball. You quickly become frustrated—it's the third time you've been hit with no foul called. You want to give the closest ref a piece of your mind, but you know that it might end up hurting your team. **WHAT WOULD YOU DO?**

Rajon Rondo talks to NBA referee Scott Foster during the 2012 playoffs.

Referees have the role of determining how a game is played and how the rules are followed. Calling a game is a difficult task, and the refs might not always make the right calls. Even so, most referees and game officials do not want players to show them up or question their calls.

To make sure their players don't get ejected, coaches will confront referees about questionable calls.

Depending on the referee, it might not take much for a player to earn a technical foul or penalty. If the player continues to argue, he or she can get **ejected** from the game or even earn a suspension. That's why most athletes try to avoid confrontations with game officials.

IN THE HEAT OF THE MOMENT

Athletes should follow three rules when dealing with referees:
- Avoid speaking to a referee when upset.
- Let the coach talk to the referee about the play.
- If you feel the need to talk to the ref about a call, do it quietly during a time-out.

Players can ask questions and ask the game official how he or she saw the play. The important thing to remember is to do it in a calm voice when the game has stopped.

FACT

Athletes are also careful how they approach officials. If they get too close, they may brush or bump an official. That can lead to an immediate ejection or suspension.

eject—to force a player or coach to leave a game

PLAYERS AND FANS

➡ *You just got sent to the penalty box during a hockey game for tripping. As you take your seat, fans from the other team immediately start taunting you and hitting the glass. You've heard it all before, but they are starting to get under your skin.* **WHAT WOULD YOU DO?**

Athletes are expected to keep their composure, even if they are being heckled by fans. They often ignore the jeering crowd and focus on doing their best. But fans have a responsibility to respect players as well. If the fans get carried away, they may get kicked out of the game.

The "green men" who attend home games for the Vancouver Canucks enjoy harassing opposing players in the penalty box.

Los Angeles Clippers guard Chris Paul signs an autograph for a young fan before a game at Staples Center.

Image matters to many athletes. Much of that image comes from fan and athlete interactions. Many players feel at ease with fans during a game. They will sign autographs, high-five fans, and wave or point to them. Fans often carry signs, give ovations, and cheer loudly for the players they love. In most cases the fan-athlete interaction is great. In 2013 Detroit Tigers first baseman Prince Fielder went into the stands to catch a foul ball. He missed the ball but was able to snag a nacho chip from a fan.

Sometimes athletes and fans take the game too seriously. Problems arise when fans and athletes frustrate each other. When this happens it's important for both the players and fans to take a step back and assess the situation. Some athletes can play along with jeering fans, but others find it harder not to react. In those moments, athletes try to remember they are playing for the love of the sport. Fans should try to remember to enjoy the sport as well and respect the athletes.

AT THE BALLPARK

Baseball and softball are games filled with close plays, where one second or one inch can make the difference. Sometimes players use techniques that help them gain an edge. These actions have become a common part of the game.

SUDDEN TIME-OUT

Time-outs are a part of most sports. In baseball a batter can call time-out to tie a shoe, check the equipment, or get additional signs from the coach. A batter can also use a time-out when a pitcher is about ready to pitch. He or she will hold up one hand to signal the ump for a time-out. While it's common for a batter to call a time-out, the pitcher might not appreciate it. It can throw off the pitcher's rhythm. In fact, umpires don't have to permit a time-out if the pitcher is about to start the windup.

Los Angeles Angels outfielder Mike Trout raises his hand, signaling to the ump that he would like time called.

FRAMING PITCHES

The job of a catcher is to call a good game. Catchers manage the field and help the pitcher work the tempo of the game. When a pitch comes in just outside the strike zone, the catcher might "frame" the pitch. As the ball hits the mitt, the catcher moves the glove quickly and slightly into the strike zone. The catcher is trying to get the strike call from the ump, and the extra time framing the pitch puts the pressure on.

HIT BY A PITCH?

A batter is awarded first base if he or she is hit by a pitch. However, some players have been questioned about the hits they take. Batters are expected to move when a ball comes close to them. If a batter is hit while hovering over the strike zone, he or she can be called out.

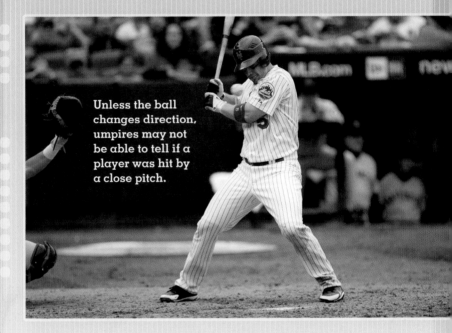

Unless the ball changes direction, umpires may not be able to tell if a player was hit by a close pitch.

Some batters try to get a free base without getting hit at all. They try to convince the umpire that the pitch hit them. New York Yankees shortstop Derek Jeter faked getting hit in a 2010 game against the Tampa Bay Rays. He was awarded first base, much to the dismay of Joe Maddon, the Rays' manager. Maddon was ejected from the game for arguing the call. Television replays showed Jeter was not hit by the pitch, which Jeter later admitted.

CHAPTER 3

Pressure to Succeed

ALTERING EQUIPMENT

➡ *You're sitting in the dugout before a softball game. You check your helmet, bat, and other equipment when a teammate walks in. She shows you a bat she just bought. She tells you it's a corked bat that will help her crush the ball. She offers to let you use the bat during the game as long as you don't tell anyone.* **WHAT WOULD YOU DO?**

It's natural to feel pressure to succeed in sports. The competition is high, and each athlete is trying to do his or her best. Players strive to become better athletes by training and practicing. Some players, though, might use unethical ways to get an advantage over their competition.

Players sometimes try to get ahead by playing with illegal equipment. Making simple changes to equipment can make the difference in a game. A bat could contain a substance to hit the ball farther. A hockey player might use a stick with a blade that has an illegal curve. A golf club could be made of prohibited materials. Game officials don't always check the equipment before a game, so some players think they can get away with it.

Minnesota Twins pitcher Joe Niekro was ejected from a 1987 game after getting caught with ball-altering materials.

Joe Niekro, a famous knuckleball pitcher, was accused of altering a baseball during a 1987 game. When the umpire asked him to empty his pockets, an emery board and sandpaper fell out. The umpires believed he had used the tools to alter the baseball. In 1982 Hall of Fame pitcher Gaylord Perry was suspended 10 games for throwing an illegal spitball against the Boston Red Sox. The umpire found petroleum jelly on the ball. Perry later admitted to using many substances, such as saliva, sweat, and dirt, to alter baseballs. The illegal substances gave the balls more movement on the pitches.

Umpires and coaches inspect a broken bat that was discovered to be corked. A corked bat is lighter and can be swung faster without sacrificing power.

PERFORMANCE-ENHANCING
DRUGS

Athletes strive to succeed, but sometimes they fall short of their goals. Many times players will change diets and exercise routines or hire trainers to help them improve. Some players turn to substances that can temporarily help their performance. These substances are called performance-enhancing drugs (PEDs). The two most common PEDs are steroids and human growth hormone (HGH). While some PEDs are used for medical conditions, some athletes use them to get an athletic advantage.

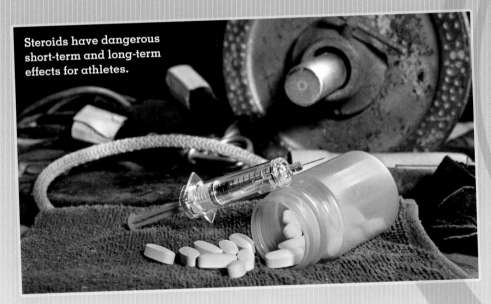

Steroids have dangerous short-term and long-term effects for athletes.

The dangers of PEDs far outweigh the benefits. There are many long-term risks of using PEDs, including high blood pressure, heart and liver problems, aggressive behavior, and depression. Players can get hooked on the drugs and develop an **addiction**. Players should never take PEDs unless their doctor prescribes them. Even then athletes should be careful not to take more than the recommended doses.

BLOOD DOPING

Some athletes use blood doping to get an advantage. Doping occurs when an athlete is preparing for a race. One of the most common methods of blood doping involves having blood removed. The athlete removes the blood when he or she is not training, which is when blood is freshest. The blood is stored and then replaced right before an event. The athlete's blood is now loaded with red blood cells, which help the body use oxygen better. Some athletes partake in blood doping even though it is prohibited. Blood doping can cause blood clots, heart attacks, or **strokes**.

Professional cycling is one of the most common sports in which athletes have admitted to blood doping.

addiction—a dependence on a drug or other substance

stroke—a problem in the brain causing a sudden loss of the ability to feel or move

ACADEMICS

➡ *Suppose you were having a tough time passing your science class. You know that getting a poor grade might stop you from playing on the soccer team. If your grade drops, you might be declared* **academically ineligible***. That means you can't play a sport until you improve your grades. You might miss the rest of the season and even lose a scholarship to your college.* **WHAT WOULD YOU DO?**

Some athletes think they have to take a shortcut to do well in school. They might ask people to cheat on tests or do homework for them. Athletes caught cheating can get in trouble for **academic fraud**.

Instead, coaches and teachers encourage athletes to show the same hard work in classes that they put into their sports. Many athletes spend extra time studying. They talk to a teacher and get extra help. Some players attend study sessions or spend time with a **tutor**. Most schools and colleges offer extra help to all students who need it, not just athletes.

Players work to keep their grades up by setting aside extra time for studying and tutoring.

Doing well in school is important for athletes. While some students become professional athletes, most will rely on their education to make a career. That's why it's important to keep a balance between academics and athletics. By working hard and putting school first, student athletes can find success on and off the field.

academically ineligible—not allowed to play a sport because of poor grades

academic fraud—the practice of cheating to get better grades

tutor—someone who provides extra help for students outside of school

PREPARING
FOR THE GAME

➡ *You just made the football team. You're still a little nervous as you get ready for the first game of the year. You know how to play the game and have showed your skill. But as you walk into the first day of meetings, you wonder how you should prepare for the game.* **WHAT WOULD YOU DO?**

Asking your coach or teammates for advice is a good place to start. Preparing for the game is just as important as playing in the game. Track athlete John Smith once said, "Success is measured by what we have done to prepare for competition."

The coach will likely show you how to properly prepare for the game. You will study plays and run through them on the field. You will run through drills and discuss what to do in certain game situations, such as a two-minute drill in football.

Coaches help players prepare for upcoming games by practicing plays, running through drills, and working through various game situations.

Oakland Athletics pitcher Dan Straily watches videotape of Toronto Blue Jays hitters before an upcoming series.

You might watch videos to prepare for the game as well. There are some types of video, though, that can't be used. Most leagues have made it clear that teams cannot videotape other teams during a practice. That might give a team an unfair advantage when preparing to play an opponent. They could learn a team's new plays or figure out signals used by the coaches.

Instead, coaches and players watch videos made during previous games. That way they can try to learn how a team plays, such as what plays a football team performs during a certain **formation**. They also study the strengths and weaknesses of individual players. Coaches can use the information to develop a game plan and help players practice.

formation—the position of football players before a snap

AGE LIMITS

➡ *You are preparing for an event as a singles figure skater several weeks before a competition. You are about to take the ice for your first warm-up when a teammate arrives to practice. You start talking, and she confides to you that she is only 13. She has her heart set on competing, but you know there are age restrictions for figure skating.* **WHAT WOULD YOU DO?**

Many sports organizations have age limits for athletes. Age limits are used for the safety of the players. Athletes who are too young might be forced to train too hard for a sport. Likewise, they might not be ready to perform actions that older athletes rely on. Some of the skills needed for a sport may cause harm to young athletes.

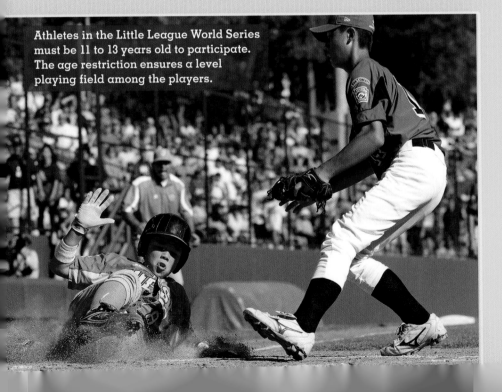

Athletes in the Little League World Series must be 11 to 13 years old to participate. The age restriction ensures a level playing field among the players.

The Olympics do not have age restrictions, but many of the events have a group that governs the competition. Some of these groups have age requirements. For example, Olympic gymnasts must be at least 16 during the year they compete, and divers have to be 14 or older. Figure skaters must be at least 15 years old before Olympic competition. Most countries tend to follow these age requirements, though there have been questions about the ages of some competitors.

At age 20 China's Cheng Fei helped her team win the gold in gymnastics at the 2008 Summer Olympics.

CHAPTER 4

Stories of Sportsmanship

➡ *It's the last play of a high school football game, and your team is down by four points. You streak down the side of the field and look back for the pass. You jump high and secure the ball with both hands in the end zone. As you start celebrating, the referee indicates you didn't land in bounds. The next day after watching video of the game, the referee admits he made the wrong call.* **HOW WOULD YOU REACT?**

A similar situation happened during a baseball game on June 2, 2010. Detroit Tigers pitcher Armando Galarraga was pitching the game of his life. He had held the Cleveland Indians hitless into the ninth inning. In fact, he didn't allow one Cleveland player to reach base. With one more out, he would have a perfect game.

On the next play, Cleveland's Jason Donald hit a ground ball to first baseman Miguel Cabrera. Cabrera threw the ball to Galarraga, who was covering the bag. It was a close play, but umpire Jim Joyce called

Slow-motion replays showed that Galarraga caught the ball before Donald's foot touched the base.

After the game Joyce saw a replay of Donald's hit. He realized he made an error on the call. He said, "I just cost that kid a perfect game."

Joyce, often voted as a popular umpire with players, apologized to Galarraga. The pitcher didn't blame Joyce, but instead thanked him for the apology. What could have easily become an ugly encounter instead became a hallmark of sportsmanship.

Galarraga and Joyce shared a handshake on the field the day after the near-perfect game.

PLAYING BY THE RULES

➡ *You hit the ball into the woods during a golf match. You are about to hit the ball back onto the fairway when your foot finds a root and you kick the golf ball by accident. You look around. No one saw that you kicked the golf ball. But you know the rules. If you kick a golf ball, it counts as a stroke against you.* **WHAT WOULD YOU DO?**

It may be hard for an athlete to tell when he or she has broken a rule, especially when no one has noticed. Many athletes, though, have come forward to tell that they broke a rule. One well-known incident occurred in the 1932 Olympics. Judy Guinness was one of the best fencers in the world. At the Summer Olympics in Los Angeles, Guinness seemed sure to win the gold medal. She came in first, but after the match, she informed officials that her opponent, Ellen Preis, actually had touched her twice. Guinness could have kept quiet, but she believed that honesty was the best policy for the games. As a result, Guinness settled for the silver medal.

Ellen Preis was awarded the gold medal in fencing at the 1932 Summer Olympics.

A similar event occurred in 2005 at the Ohio state golf championship. Adam Van Houten noticed his playing partner made an error on the scorecard. The card showed that Van Houten had scored a 5 on a hole, but it was actually a 6. Van Houten had already signed his card. Because it was signed, he would be disqualified if he told game officials about the error. To Van Houten, honesty was more important than winning. He informed officials of the error, and he was disqualified. *Sports Illustrated* honored him by including him on the top 10 list for best sportsmanship of the decade.

SPORTSMANSHIP IN ACTION

One of the most famous stories of sportsmanship occurred in the 1956 Australian National Championships. The race helped determine who would run for the country in the Summer Olympics later that year. Australian John Landy was running in a 1,500-meter race. During the race fellow runner Ron Clarke fell. Landy tried to jump over him, but he hit Clarke with his cleat, cutting him. Landy stopped to make sure Clarke was fine. Landy then passed all the runners, coming in first at 4 minutes, 4 seconds. He didn't meet his personal goal, but he showed true sportsmanship that day.

FACT
Landy is still considered a hero in his home country of Australia. He even served as governor of the territory of Victoria from 2001 to 2006.

John Landy

Arden McMath (left) and Meghan Vogel

CROSSING THE FINISH LINE

In 2012 Meghan Vogel was running in the Ohio Division III State Championships. As a junior for West Liberty-Salem High School, she had already won the 1,600-meter title. She was hoping to score another win in the 3,200-meter race.

Tired from the first race, Vogel fell off championship pace. She was rounding the last leg when Arden McMath, a runner from another team, fell to the track. Vogel knew something was wrong. Instead of continuing the race, Vogel helped McMath to her feet and helped her complete the last 20 yards to the finish line. She even made sure McMath finished before her.

Luz Long (left) and Jesse Owens talk before the long jump at the 1936 Summer Olympics.

Many players have helped opponents succeed, even at the risk of losing. In the 1936 Olympics, Luz Long was a star long jumper for Germany. He hoped to wow the home crowd of his country's capital, Berlin, which hosted the Olympics. When performing in qualifiers, he paid careful attention to one of his competitors, Jesse Owens. He noticed that the American was having trouble with his jumps. Owens' first two jumps in a qualifier ended in fouls. A third foul would prevent him from competing any further.

Some sources say Long went over to Owens and advised he move his jumping point. The advice worked, and Owens advanced in the qualifier. He eventually beat out Long in the Olympics and won the gold medal. Despite the rise of Nazi dictator Adolf Hitler and his belief in Aryan supremacy, Long embraced Owens after he won.

FACT

Luz Long was killed during World War II, which started three years after the Olympics. Long's family and Owens' family remained in contact for many years.

Sportsmanship shined again when the Western Oregon women's softball team took on Central Washington in 2008. Oregon outfielder Sara Tucholsky was so excited to hit her first home run that she forgot to step on first base. She turned back toward first but hurt her right knee in the process. Central Washington first baseman Mallory Holtman realized that Tucholsky could not run. If Tucholsky got assistance from her trainer, coach, or players, she would be out. Instead, Holtman asked the umpire if she could help Tucholsky around the base. She and Washington shortstop Liz Wallace carried Holtman around the bases for her first home run.

215

Liz Wallace (from left),
Sara Tucholsky, and
Mallory Holtman

Paolo di Canio (left) received the FIFA fair play award at a 2001 gala in Zurich, Switzerland.

STOPPING PLAY

In 2000 West Ham United was playing Everton in a European Premier League soccer match. It was a hard-fought game, and the two teams each had one goal with time running out. Going after the ball away from the net, Everton goalie Paul Gerrard slid to block the ball. He remained on the ground while clutching his knee, leaving the goal wide open. West Ham player Paolo di Canio received a pass from a teammate and had the perfect opportunity to score.

Instead of kicking the ball for a sure goal, di Canio caught the pass with his hands. The action caused the play to stop. He waved to the sideline, motioning for help for Gerrard. The action earned di Canio a standing ovation from the crowd and an award for his sportsmanship.

ONE FOR THE RECORD BOOKS

Illinois high school quarterback Nate Haasis had the opportunity of a lifetime on October 25, 2003. With 30 more passing yards, the Southeast High School senior could set a conference record. He would also join the list of high school players who have passed for 5,000 yards. But time was running out.

Down by 16 with less than a minute to play, Haasis led his team down the field. He threw one final pass for 37 yards, securing the conference record in passing yards. After the game Haasis found out that the coaches of both teams had made a deal. Southeast would allow its opponent to score toward the end of the game. Then the other team would play easy on Haasis and let him break the passing record.

Haasis didn't feel right about claiming the record. He wrote to the conference president, stating he didn't want the record the way he earned it. His name was removed from the record, but Haasis was applauded for his ethical decision.

ETHICS AND SPORTSMANSHIP

Competition and fair play are at the heart of all sports. When athletes behave ethically and follow the rules of sportsmanship, great things can happen. Playing fair takes dedication, hard work, and commitment. Try your best and enjoy what you're doing. In the end, you'll have your own personal success.

GLOSSARY

academically ineligible—not allowed to play a sport because of poor grades

academic fraud—the practice of cheating to get better grades

addiction—a dependence on a drug or other substance

blowout—a game in which one team greatly outscores its opponent

concussion—an injury to the brain caused by a hard blow to the head

eject—to force a player or coach to leave a game

flop—falling in order to trick the referee into calling a foul

formation—the position of football players before a snap

penalty—a punishment for breaking the rules of a game

rivalry—a fierce feeling of competition between two players or teams

sportsmanship—fair and respectful behavior when playing a sport

stroke—a problem in the brain causing a sudden loss of the ability to feel or move

time-out—a pause taken during a game that can be called by a team member or game official

tutor—someone who provides extra help for students outside of school

READ MORE

Butterfield, Moira. *The Olympics: Scandals*. Mankato, Minn.: Sea to Sea Publications, 2011.

Golus, Carrie. *Jim Thorpe. Sports Heroes and Legends*. Minneapolis: Twenty-First Century Books, 2007.

Herzog, Brad. *Inspiring Stories of Sportsmanship*. Minneapolis: Free Spirit Publishing, 2014.

Hunter, Nick. *Sportsmanship*. Chicago: Heinemann Library, 2012.

INTERNET SITES

FactHound offers a safe, fun way to find Internet sites related to this book. All of the sites on FactHound have been researched by our staff.

Here's all you do:

Visit *www.facthound.com*

Type in this code: 9781476541532

Super-cool stuff!

Check out projects, games and lots more at
www.capstonekids.com

INDEX